Any Time, LORD

Honest Prayers for MOTHERS

Jeanie Gibson

St. Paul Books & Media

Library of Congress Cataloging-in-Publication Data

Gibson, Jeanie.
     Any time, Lord.

     1. Mothers—Prayer-books and devotions—English.
I. Title.
BX2170.M65G53   1988   242'.8431   87-30510
ISBN 0-8198-0732-X (pbk.)

Printed in the U.S.A., by the Daughters of St. Paul
50 St. Paul's Ave., Boston, MA 02130

The Daughters of St. Paul are an international congregation of women
religious serving the Church with the communications media.

Contents

Dedicated to
all mothers everywhere
who transmit life and make it so beautiful

Introduction

There is a very poignant scene in *Miracle of Marcelino,* a film about an orphaned boy who asks his Special Friend, "What is a *mother?"* Jesus replies that a mother is someone who "gives" of herself. She is someone who spends herself for others.

"Do *you* have a mother?" little Marcelino asks.

"Yes," Jesus replies with great love—the same love with which he bequeathed her from the cross to all mankind.

Obviously, there is no other mother who has given more than Mary, from the moment she gave her *"Fiat"* to the Angel Gabriel to that harrowing scene at Calvary when Jesus said to the Apostle John, "Behold your Mother." It is no wonder that, through all the intervening centuries, she has been the model of motherhood.

When we read Scripture, we find that the Blessed Mother was quite immersed in and aware of the *realities* in her life. She first questioned the angel as to *how* she could be pregnant when she had not "known" a man. She *pondered* the prophesies uttered when she and Joseph took the Infant Savior to the Temple for the prescribed circumcision, and no doubt wondered at Simeon's words about a "sword piercing her heart." Also, when Jesus, at the age of twelve, was lost for three days, we can safely conjecture that she was *deeply* distressed before finding him in the Temple.

Those of us who are mothers can have a special identification with the Mother of God as *we* live out the realities of our state in life—be they joys, sorrows, frustrations or human frailty. Like Mary, moreover, we need to have a "gut honesty" when we bring these things to God in prayer.

9

Jeanie Gibson has done precisely this in her book. She has brought to our Lord the everyday concerns of a modern mother. In the light of Scripture and other writings, she has reflected on a wide variety of personal and family situations—and in the process has given readers much that they can ponder.

Most of us have no difficulty identifying with her prayers about forgiveness, good parenting, being our "neighbor's keeper," thanksgiving, and learning how to pray in "the chapel of the heart." In addition, a good many more will give an understanding nod when she speaks to the Lord about the effort "to stay in love" and the pain of feeling unappreciated, a time when one must fight against a "collection agency" attitude.

Then there are all those cultural lures which entice or perplex today's Christians: dieting, staying young, getting through incredibly busy days, coping with financial worries—and trying to look beautiful! As the author so convincingly shows us, however, *all* of what makes up our day-to-day life must be seen through a spiritual window. It must be measured by the yardstick of God's Word.

We can almost imagine the Lord smiling at some tell-it-like-it-is prayers of hers—such as "The Three 'P's"—or his loving forgiveness when she makes a humble confession of faults and sins in "Living by My Own Standards."

In a society where there is almost exclusive emphasis on "getting" rather than "giving," Jeanie Gibson's prayers help to point the way for today's mothers. It is refreshing to note that others are also trying to be *in* the world but not *of* the world.

—Mary Drahos

Daybreak

It is always springtime
in the heart
that loves God.

St. John Vianney

Daybreak

Dear God,
Your golden sun is streaming through
my kitchen window.
The warm rays remind me
that Your love surrounds my life.

This day is fresh and new and beautiful,
a precious gift of Your love.
Let me live it in serenity,
patience, joy, trust, goodness,
unselfishness, faith and love.
May I meet the opportunities of this day
with optimism and courage.
May I bear the trials with meekness and fortitude,
and may I accomplish some good today
that will make others happier
and myself better prepared for life with You
in the glory of heaven.

My heart is steadfast
    O God, my heart is steadfast!
I will sing and make melody!
    Awake, my soul!

Awake, O harp and lyre!
    I will awake the dawn!
I will give thanks to you, O Lord, among the
        peoples,
    I will sing praises to you among the nations.
For your steadfast love is great above the heavens,
    your faithfulness reaches to the clouds. *(Ps 108:1-4)*

Trying to Understand

*If you have
anything of good,
believe better things
of others, that you
may preserve humility.*

Thomas à Kempis

Trying to Understand

Lord,
I often find it hard to understand
some things that are so important to others
and so small according to my way
of looking at things.
You've made us all so different,
unique expressions of Your image,
individual reflections of Your goodness.
Help me, Lord, to be humble enough
to appreciate differences,
and never to brush them off rashly.
I almost choke to admit it,
but deep down I know
that there are times when my viewpoints
are really not the best.
Let me learn to swallow wounding words
and instead to treat others
as I would treat You.
Seeing eye to eye with everyone
is impossible, I know.
But seeing through differences
to the "sameness" of humanity
is a gift of grace
that can rouse compassion,
gentleness and goodness.
Help my eyesight, Lord.
Let me understand others
as I myself want to be understood.

Perform your tasks in meekness;
     then you will be loved
by those whom God accepts.
The greater you are,
     the more you must humble yourself;
     so you will find favor in the sight of the Lord.
For great is the might of the Lord;
     he is glorified by the humble.
Seek not what is too difficult for you,
     nor investigate what is beyond your power.
Reflect upon what has been assigned to you,
     for you do not need what is hidden.
Do not meddle in what is beyond your tasks,
     for matters too great for human understanding
          have been shown you.
For their hasty judgment has led many astray,
     and wrong opinion
          has caused their thoughts to slip. *(Sir 3:17-24)*

Friendship

There is no
true friendship
unless you weld it
between souls
who cleave together
through that love
which is shed
in our hearts
by the Holy Spirit
who is given to us.

St. Augustine

Friendship

Dear Lord,
my God and my Friend,
there is an art that I need
special help with:
the art of keeping friends.

Misunderstandings are so easy to begin
and often so hard to end.
Sometimes it seems that circumstances
contrive to make life and relationships
a series of potholes to be missed.
But I am grateful that
in this challenging undertaking
of making and keeping friends
You are the perfect example.

How You loved Your closest friends, the apostles!
You sought to bring out the best in them,
to encourage when they were down,
to provide for their deepest needs,
to share Your thoughts and to listen to theirs.
Never was there a time
when You denied them some good
because of self-interest.
Your friendship was proven in deeds,
in down-on-Your-knees service,
in up-on-the-cross sacrifice.

Teach me, Lord,
to be a friend to each and to all.
Let me recognize in each person
a friend already made
or a friend still to be gained.
And may each friendship be based on
a lasting, genuine relationship with You,
the one who gives meaning
to every true friendship.

A faithful friend is a sturdy shelter:
    he that has found one has found a treasure.
There is nothing so precious as a faithful friend,
    And no scales can measure his excellence.
A faithful friend is an elixir of life;
    and those who fear the Lord will find him.
Whoever fears the Lord directs his friendship aright,
    for as he is, so is his neighbor also. *(Sir 6:14-17)*

The Struggle to Forgive

To err is human,
to forgive divine.

Alexander Pope

The Struggle to Forgive

Lord,
if this were the first time
that I'd been hurt so deeply
I think I would be able
to forget more quickly.
But that "70 times 7" figure You mentioned
seems to be getting closer and closer....

Yes, Lord, I know the number is symbolic
and means I must forgive always.
But it certainly is hard to do that
when offenses are repeated
and hurts are renewed.

Make me, Lord, at least a little like You.
I treasure Your forgiveness
and benefit from Your mercy.
Yet I do not feel inclined sometimes
to imitate Your goodness.

If the feelings won't go away,
please still let my will be firmly set
on "turning the other cheek,"
on being unselfish,
on forgiving so that I might also be forgiven.

"Forgive us our debts,
    As we have forgiven our debtors." *(Mt 6:12)*

"For if you forgive men their trespasses,
    your heavenly Father also will forgive you." *(Mt 6:14)*

Put on then, as God's chosen ones, holy and
beloved, compassion, kindness, lowliness, meekness,
and patience, forbearing one another and, if one
has a complaint against another, forgiving each
other; as the Lord has forgiven you, so you also
must forgive. And above all these put on love,
which binds everything together in perfect harmony.

(Col 3:12-14)

Beauty

What beauty lies hidden
in the wisdom of God!
From it alone
do all things
derive that beauty
which appeals to our eyes.
But to see that beauty,
to embrace it, our hearts
have to be purified.

St. Augustine

Beauty

Dear God,
I've just met one of the most beautiful persons
I've ever had the pleasure of encountering.
Her hair, her eyes, her mouth, her bearing...
these were not the things that made her stunning.
Rather, the gentle goodness,
the thoughtful unselfishness,
the unpretentious manner,
the good-natured attitude—
these traits have carved a profound imprint
on my memory.

How beautiful You must be, Lord,
if Your dim reflection in a human being
can be so appealing.
How tragic it is when "beauty"
is considered something external.

Unfortunately, I have often fallen into the trap
of looking superficially at beauty.
Pretty clothes, lovely furniture, attractive features
—appealing "things."
But real beauty is found only in You, Lord,
and in mirroring Your perfection.
Considering beauty as only "external"
is as sensible as trying to appreciate
the taste of fruit
by looking at the color of its peel.

Help me, Lord, to see Your beauty everywhere,
to sense Your creative hand in events,
circumstances, things and people.
Enable me to replace the "ugliness" of sin
in my life
with the splendor of reflecting Your goodness.
Then I shall not only see
but also share more fully
the Beauty You are.

The Mighty One, God the Lord,
    speaks and summons the earth
    from the rising of the sun to its setting.
Out of Zion, the perfection of beauty,
    God shines forth. (Ps 50:1-2)

Let not yours be the outward adorning..., but let it
be the hidden person of the heart with the
imperishable jewel of a gentle and quiet spirit,
which in God's sight is very precious. (1 Pt 3:3, 4)

The Newcomer

*A child is a pledge
of immortality,
for he bears
upon him in figure
those high and eternal
excellences in which
the joy of heaven
consists....*

John H. Cardinal Newman

The Newcomer

Lord,
the months of expectation are over
and I have held near my heart
the precious bundle of my first child.
Every feature, every movement,
every whimper is etched into my being.

Thank You, Lord.
How wondrous are Your works!
And none more wondrous
than Your image in this innocent one.

Make me every bit a mother...
something like the perfect Mother
You chose for Your own.
How I want her gentle, loving manner
to be a part of my life,
a model for my motherhood.

As You, Lord, have entrusted
the priceless gift of a human being
into the hands of my husband and me
so now I offer this little one to You.
Never let me forget that he is Your son too,
and that as a parent my greatest duty
is to help this child grow in Your life.
May I also have the joy of someday sharing
with You and with him
and with all my loved ones
the everlasting life of glory.

What is man that you are mindful of him,
    and the son of man that you care for him?
Yet you have made him little less than God,
    and crown him with glory and honor. (Ps 8:4-5)

And [the shepherds] went with haste, and found
Mary and Joseph, and the babe lying in a
manger.... But Mary kept all these things, pondering
them in her heart. (Lk 2:16, 19)

Learning
from
Mistakes

*Those who do things
make mistakes.
Those who do nothing
live a mistake.*

Servant of God,
James Alberione

Learning from Mistakes

Dear God,
I've done it again.
Will I ever learn not to speak before I reflect,
not to act before I think things over?
I wish there could be an eraser in life
to remove the blotches and the scribbles.
Your forgiveness is the greatest consolation in life.
Thanks for understanding, Lord.

I am also starting to see
that even from my bungles good can be derived.
Let me learn from my mistakes, O Lord,
not for fear of humiliation,
but because You will that I grow in Your likeness.
You gave me a mind for learning,
a will for trying,
a heart for loving,
emotions for channeling,
and physical strength for acting in Your name.
Please, Lord, don't let me get bogged down
in the mire of pessimism and defeatism.
Give me the perception to discover my weaknesses,
the humility to try to change
and the confidence to trust in Your grace
which is made perfect in weakness.

The fear of the Lord is the beginning of knowledge;
    fools despise wisdom and instruction. *(Prv 1:7)*

He said to me, "My grace is sufficient for you, for my power is made perfect in weakness." I will all the more gladly boast of my weaknesses, that the power of Christ may rest upon me. *(2 Cor 12:9)*

We do not have a high priest who is unable to sympathize with our weaknesses, but one who in every respect has been tempted as we are, yet without sinning. Let us then with confidence draw near to the throne of grace, that we may receive mercy and find grace to help in time of need.

(Heb 5:15-16)

Recipe for a Spiritual Coffee Break!

1 mind (calm or willing to become so)
1 mustard seed of faith
2 wills (God's and ours)
1 ½ oz. of trust
1 heart of love
2 clasped hands (optional)
gratitude, adoration, sorrow, petition
2-5 minutes of silence

Blend ingredients, making sure that mind and faith, will and trust, heart and love are inseparable. Add mixture to God's will, so that the predominant flavor is the divine taste. For best results, make sure that the consistency is uniform.

Hands may now be clasped, but this is not essential. Place the mixture in a setting (standing, sitting or kneeling position) for two to five minutes, in a quiet place, warmed by God's burning love. Stir up sentiments of gratitude, adoration, sorrow and petition. Then drink deeply to "Taste and see that the Lord is good!" *(Ps 34:8)*

Over a Coffee Cup

Thank You, Lord,
for this time of relaxation.
It's good to just stop a moment
and have time to think and sip and pray.

Some days seem to go by
before I even know they've come.
They are almost empty days
because I let them be that way.
I "gulp" down the hours
instead of "sipping" minutes
and relishing their opportunities.
Then before I know it, the "cup" is drained
and another unrepeatable day is gone.

Lord, help me to live in the present moment.
Teach me to thirst not for accomplishment,
not for getting things over and done with
but for living my life meaningfully,
in a manner worthy of Your follower.

So many words are said over a cup of coffee,
so many opinions are exchanged,
so many "news items" shared.
It's good, Lord, to have had this coffee break
with You today.

I hope You'll help me
to remember Your presence often
during the less peaceful moments.
Know, Lord, that You are always welcome.
Drop in...any time.

As a hart longs for flowing streams,
    so longs my soul
        for you, O God.
My soul thirsts for God,
    for the living God.
When shall I come
    and behold the face of God? (Ps 42:1-2)

O taste and see that the Lord is good!
    Happy is the man who takes refuge in him!

(Ps 34:8)

Good Parenting

What is a mother?
Who shall answer this?
A mother is a font
and spring of life,
A mother is a forest
in whose heart lies hid
a secret
ancient as the hills,
For men to claim
and take its wealth away;
And like the forest
shall her wealth renew
and give, and give again,
that men may live.

Francis Joseph Cardinal Spellman

Good Parenting

Father,
how good it is to call You by that name!
It helps me to remember that You understand
what it means to have children
who depend upon You.

When You entrusted children
into our hands
You gave my husband and me
one of the greatest joys of life.
You admitted us into the wonderful work
of Your creation.
Thank You, Lord.

Now, though, as the years pass
and little feet and hands
assume new dimensions,
and young minds acquire
new knowledge and attitudes,
help us to be understanding and loving,
patient and attentive,
alert to needs and perceptive of potentials.
Enable us to guide without dominating,
to inspire without preaching,
to love without demanding,
to challenge without burdening,
to communicate without prying,
and to trust without being imprudent.

Father of us all,
help us to recognize the marvel
of individual differences
and to appreciate uniqueness
more than success or achievement.

May our children, who are Yours first of all,
be brought closer to You daily
because they see in their parents
a reflection of their heavenly Father.

Come, O sons, listen to me,
   I will teach you the fear of the Lord. *(Ps 34:11)*

Those who trust in him will understand truth, and
the faithful will abide with him in love, because
grace and mercy are upon his elect, and he watches
over his holy ones. *(Wis 3:9)*

Aim at righteousness, godliness, faith, love,
steadfastness, gentleness. *(1 Tim 6:11)*

Not Worrying

*In His will
is perfected our peace.*
Dante

Not Worrying

Lord,
I'd like to think that I trust You.
But so often I catch myself
worrying and worrying and worrying some more.
"What if...?" and "What if...?"
It's like a haunting, taunting habit.

I know that worrying
is quite different from concern.
I'm concerned about my husband and children
and that's a right attitude.
But I worry needlessly about nonessentials,
and that's a waste of precious time and thought.

I once read a saying
that went something like this:
    Worrying is like a rocking chair—
    It gives you plenty to do
    But gets you nowhere.
There's wisdom in those lines

Help me, Lord, to take life in stride,
to quit pretending that
the worst thing possible is bound to happen.
Let me remain calm because You are directing
every moment of my life.

Even when there's a storm,
and You appear to be sleeping,
there is bound to be safety
as long as You are present
in the little boat of my life.
Let the winds howl, Lord.
Let the waves lash.
If You are near, so too is peace.

"Fear not, little flock, for it is your Father's good
pleasure to give you the kingdom." (Lk 12:32)

And a great storm of wind arose, and the waves
beat into the boat, so that the boat was already
filling. But he was in the stern, asleep on the
cushion; and they woke him and said to him,
"Teacher do you not care if we perish?" And he
awoke and rebuked the wind, and said to the sea,
"Peace! Be still!" And the wind ceased, and there
was a great calm. He said to them, "Why are you
afraid? Have you no faith?" (Mk 4:37-40)

Living by My Own Standards

*The business
of finding fault
is very easy
and that of doing better
very hard.*

St. Francis de Sales

Living by
My Own Standards

O God,
I have to admit that it's much easier
to demand than to witness.
I guess I've got a good dose of phariseeism,
because I find it much more convenient
to require goodness of others
and to expect virtue from them
than to live up myself to the standards
I find in Your Gospel.
It can get pretty tough
to be all that a Christian really must be,
to be all that I exact from family and friends.

Give me a new heart, O Lord.
No one is greater than You
and yet You ask of us only those things
which are for our good.
You meet us where we're at,
forgive us when we fail,
help us to improve
and strengthen us for the task.
You don't scold, put on airs, or belittle,
but You encourage and elevate
because You are love.
Let me learn to overlook others' shortcomings, Lord,
and to focus instead
on being what You want me to be.

"Judge not, that you be not judged. For with the judgment you pronounce you will be judged, and the measure you give will be the measure you get. Why do you see the speck that is in your brother's eye, but do not notice the log that is in your own eye?" *(Mt 7:1-3)*

"You are the light of the world. A city set on a hill cannot be hid. Nor do men light a lamp and put it under a bushel, but on a stand, and it gives light to all in the house. Let your light so shine before men, that they may see your good works and give glory to your Father who is in heaven." *(Mt 5:14-16)*

Measles, Mumps and Flu

They do not love
that do not show
their love.

John Heywood

Measles, Mumps and Flu

Hello, Lord.
This is Dr. Mother calling in.
The fever's down, thank goodness,
but I sure was worried for a while.

It's at times like these, Lord,
that I think back to all the occasions
when I myself needed care and attention.
It's no fun getting up at 2:00 A.M.
to give medicine,
and I'm sure it wasn't the thrill of my mother's life
to do the same for me the fourth time
I got measles.
Life takes its twists and turns, doesn't it, Lord?
It seems like yesterday
that I was in the sick bed,
unhappy about the flu,
but pleasantly resigned that I'd be missing school.
Now my own children
have inherited my ability to catch every "bug"
that comes within a fifty-mile radius.
When I was their age, I simply took it for granted
that Mom would wait on me hand and foot,
would be absolutely concerned and understanding
and would show not the least sign of impatience
until my recovery was full and complete.
I can't say that I've always been
the most patient Dr. Mother
on the earth's surface, Lord.

Sometimes the demands of ten-year-olds
make me wonder if Job could have survived
with them.

Yet, Lord, I know
that with Your help all is possible.
Let me grow healthier spiritually today
by seeing You in the little people I serve
and loving You in them
whether they be well and lively
or sick and a bit grumpy.

Love is patient and kind; love is not jealous or
boastful; it is not arrogant or rude. Love does not
insist on its own way; it is not irritable or resentful;
it does not rejoice at wrong, but rejoices in the
right. Love bears all things, believes all things,
hopes all things, endures all things. So faith, hope,
love abide, these three; but the greatest of these is
love. *(1 Cor 13:4-7, 13)*

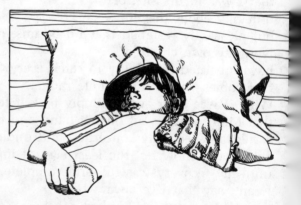

Finances

Build not thine house
on height up to the sky.
None falleth far,
but he that climbeth high.
Remember, Nature
sent you hither bare:
the gifts of fortune—
count them
borrowed ware.

St. Thomas More

Finances

Dear Lord,
You appreciated the gift of the widow's mite,
taught that the poor in spirit are blessed
and witnessed from Bethlehem to Calvary
that poverty is pleasing to Your Father.
Help our family to put our spiritual needs first
and to be less material minded.
How difficult it is to learn the lesson
that happiness is not found
in having what we want
but in wanting what we have.
Sales are like bait,
and it's easy to swallow
hook, line and sinker.
It's all too possible
to become possessed by possessions,
to be preoccupied by financial needs
to the point of losing sight
of the goods that last forever.

Let our hearts be fixed on heavenly treasures,
while using earthly goods wisely
and sharing with those less privileged
than ourselves.
Help us to remember that You are the Giver
and we are only stewards.
Some day what You have entrusted to us
You will ask an account of.

Lord, increase in us
a trust in Your Providence.
You promised You'd never leave us
lacking in anything we really need.
We trust You, Lord. Help us trust You more.

"Do not lay up for yourselves treasures on earth, where moth and rust consume and where thieves break in and steal, but lay up for yourselves treasures in heaven, where neither moth nor rust consumes and where thieves do not break in and steal. For where your treasure is, there will your heart be also." *(Mt 6:19-21)*

To Overcome Frustration

*Patient endurance is
the perfection
of love.*
St. Ambrose

To Overcome Frustration

Dear Lord,
it seems so much goes into
being a parent.
Yet it also appears that so little
is recognized as being well intentioned,
as being motivated by love and concern.

When my children were younger
I puzzled them when I took them away
from that intriguing medicine cabinet
and removed their itching fingers
from anything that could change
curiosity into tragedy.

Now the poison I warn them of
is the allurement of immoral media,
the pull of "what everyone is doing,"
the attraction of drug and drink.

Still they look at me with disbelief,
as though I were trying to transport them
back in time,
as though I were unaware of the rapid changes
that society has experienced
and is continuing to undergo.

Help me, Lord, to resist my inclination
to succumb to the pouts and sullen looks.
Preserve me from the temptation
to consider my children's lives

as a sculpturing of my own hands
rather than Your work of art,
effected with parents' help
but not solely through their efforts.

I am tempted at times to be frustrated,
to expect more of them
because I recall how much my husband and I
have tried to give.
Yet in my righteous wrath
I often forget that You have given far more to me
and I have often repaid so scantily.

Just as You have never given up on me, Lord,
so let me never lose faith in my children.
Let me never pretend that I can take
full credit—or full blame—
for what they are or shall be.

Make me perceptive enough
to recognize "stages" in their growth,
and patient enough to endure the behavior
which I can't understand
and the rejection they sometimes evidence
toward things I hold dear.

You who are so patient with my growing in love,
help me to overcome frustration
with a deepening trust in Your grace.
Let nothing rob me of a gentle goodness
that will reflect the mercy I have received from You.

Give ear to my prayer, O God;
    and hide not yourself from my supplication!
Attend to me, and answer me;
    I am overcome by my trouble.
It is not an enemy who taunts me—
    then I could bear it;
it is not an adversary who deals insolently
        with me—
    then I could hide from him.
But I call upon God;
    and the Lord will save me. *(Ps 55:1-2, 12, 16)*

After a Busy Day

*We must measure
our trials by ourself,
And not ourself
by our trials.*

St. John of the Cross

*There is nothing
that we suffer
for the honor of God,
however little it may be,
that is not more
serviceable to us
than if we possessed
the dominion of the world.*

Archbishop William B. Ullathorne

After a Busy Day

Lord, I don't know how I survived today.

My first mistake was waking up,
and my second was not going back to sleep.
But life's demands can't be shut off
as easily as a buzzing alarm clock.
So today I've rushed to prepare meals,
scrambled to the orthodontist's,
scurried through shopping,
dashed to deliver my thirteen-year-old baseball star
to his practice,
and have not had a moment to breathe
in between it all.

You, Lord, are the only calmness
in my crowded, hectic life.
But often I'm blind to Your light,
deaf to Your reassuring voice
and forgetful of Your promise to be with me.

Jesus, let me never be "too busy"
to love You in myself and in others.
Help me to make my hurrying
a gift of unselfish giving,
and remind me, please,
that even on days like today
I can find joy in doing Your will.

The Lord is my shepherd, I shall not want;
    he makes me lie down in green pastures.
He leads me beside still waters;
    he restores my soul.
He leads me in paths of righteousness
    for his name's sake.

Even though I walk through the valley
        of the shadow of death,
    I fear no evil;
for you are with me;
    your rod and your staff,
    they comfort me.

You prepare a table before me
    in the presence of my enemies;
you anoint my head with oil,
    my cup overflows.
Surely goodness and mercy shall follow me
    all the days of my life;
and I shall dwell in the house of the Lord
    for ever. *(Ps 23:1-6)*

To Stay in Love

*Love can deny nothing
to love.*
Andreas Capellanus

To Stay in Love

Lord,
the honeymoon is long over,
but love must always be a new experience.
Songs make us think that love
is thrills and pleasure.
But the deepest love is that which demands
of those who love
the gift of their very selves.

Be, O Lord, the third party
in my marriage.
No love is real or enduring or deep
unless it is modeled on Yours
and found faithful as Yours
despite the inevitable cost.

As You have loved Your people
and made Yourself one with them,
let my husband and me
be united in a love that is truly interior,
a love not based upon things
but upon the sharing of our very beings—
a union of thought, of goals,
of dreams, of convictions.

Teach me to speak when words are the solution,
to keep silent when silence is the best answer,
to smile when a smile will soothe,
to forgive when forgiveness will heal.

Let me never exchange love
for the desire to dominate
or to reap satisfaction
or to receive when I should give.

Lord, may the love You have blessed
between my husband and me
be a reflection of Your love
today and every day
until we enter the kingdom of eternal love.

My soul takes pleasure in three things,
    and they are beautiful in the sight of the Lord
       and of men:
agreement between brothers, friendship between
      neighbors,
    and a wife and husband who live in harmony.
(Sir 25:1)

Therefore be imitators of God, as beloved children.
And walk in love, as Christ loved us and gave
himself up for us, a fragrant offering and sacrifice
to God. *(Eph 5:1-2)*

[May] their hearts be encouraged as they are knit
together in love, to have all the riches of assured
understanding and the knowledge of God's mystery,
of Christ, in whom are hid all the treasures of
wisdom and knowledge. *(Col 2:2-3)*

My Neighbor's Keeper

Charity is the pure gold
which makes us rich
in eternal wealth.

J. P. Camus

My Neighbor's Keeper

Lord,
I hear so often about the troubles of others.
It seems that there are heartache,
worry and concern
all around and in everyone.
Why, Lord?

I wonder sometimes if we'll ever understand
what there is in Your way of looking at things
that makes it so different from ours.

Just this morning I spoke with my friend
about her approaching divorce,
heard about the illness of a neighbor,
learned of the financial problems of a relative,
and discovered that a close acquaintance
has lost her son in a drunken-driving accident.

I have a hard time coping with all the bad news
that seems to surround human life.
Yet others expect of Your followers
words of encouragement,
a ready smile,
profound compassion,
genuine interest,
and a promise of prayer.

Help me, Lord, to reach out to others
without becoming desolate or downhearted.
Make my spiritual "shoulders" broad enough

to bear my own cross
and to share the burdens of others.
Open my heart to others' needs,
even when my own tend to weigh me down.
Let pain never harden me,
but instead make me ever more understanding
and gentle
towards those who need support.
Inspire me to speak and act in such a way
that others will be encouraged
to face life optimistically,
confident of Your help, especially in time of need.

Make me truly my neighbor's keeper,
not in the sense of unwarranted curiosity
or for the sake of gossip,
but so that I may mirror Your love and concern.
Then perhaps I will better see
the good that is harvested through suffering.
And I will better know You,
who became our neighbor and our brother
so that our suffering would never again be useless.

Do good to a friend...
        and reach out and give to him as much
            as you can. (Sir 14:13)

It is my prayer that your love may abound more
and more, with knowledge and all discernment, so

that you may approve what is excellent, and may be pure and blameless for the day of Christ, filled with the fruits of righteousness which come through Jesus Christ, to the glory and praise of God.

(Phil 1:9-11)

Bear one another's burdens, and so fulfill the law of Christ. *(Gal 6:2)*

Teach Me How to Pray

As down in
the sunless retreats
of the ocean,
Sweet flowers
are springing
no mortal can see,
So, deep in my soul
the still prayer
of devotion
Unheard by the world
rises silent to Thee.

Thomas Moore

Teach Me How to Pray

Dear God,
today's world is not exactly
conducive to growth in the spiritual life.
Yet being a Christian means
putting You first and advancing in that love
regardless of the "risks" involved,
the opinions of others,
or the sacrifices encountered.

Lord, teach me how to pray
when all is easy
and when all seems hard.
Let me learn to retire
into the chapel of my heart
where I can find You any time.
Give me the desire to praise You
for Your goodness, to thank You
for Your benefits,
to ask Your pardon
for my sins,
and to ask Your help
for my many needs and those of others.

Teach me, too, to listen in prayer
to the whispering of Your counsel,
to the kind invitation
that draws me to higher things.
Inspire me with a gentle spirit
that is satisfied with simply being near You,

that is happy only when Your will is fulfilled
and Your glory is achieved.

I love You, Lord,
who are always so near,
always so available to listen,
always so ready to answer.

"Pray then like this:
    'Our Father who are in heaven,
    Hallowed be your name.
    Your kingdom come,
    Your will be done,
        On earth as it is in heaven.
    'Give us this day our daily bread;
    And forgive us our debts,
        As we also have forgiven our debtors;
    And lead us not into temptation,
        But deliver us from evil.'" (Mt 6:9-13)

"Ask, and it will be given you; seek, and you will
find; knock, and it will be opened to you. For every
one who asks receives, and he who seeks finds, and
to him who knocks it will be opened." (Mt 7:7-8)

Feeling Unappreciated

*Happiness is not
a matter of events;
it depends
upon the tides
of the mind.*

Alice Meynell

Feeling Unappreciated

Lord,
I'm starting to feel
like a part of the woodwork
or a piece of the carpet.
Why is it that even persons I love
just seem to take me for granted?
I've knocked myself out,
tried to do whatever I can to show my love,
and I've received about as much recognition
as the skillet does once it's been used.

You know me, Lord.
I'm not asking for the Nobel Peace Prize.
I'm not looking for headlines or magazine covers.
But, goodness, a few more "thank you's"
or "I love you's" would certainly help me
to feel a lot more appreciated.

Is it all in my outlook, Jesus?
Have I lost sight
of the real reason for my life
and for the demands it makes on me?
Am I being unfair to others
by not being open and honest,
yet expecting them to read my thoughts
and know my inmost needs?

Lord, help me to recognize appreciation
in signs other than words.

Enable me to seek Your recognition first of all and to be satisfied with whatever other thanks may come my way.
Don't let me assume a "collection agency" attitude about repayment for the gift of my love.
As You have served, let me now minister—freely, happily, humbly.

"Beware of practicing your piety before men in order to be seen by them; for then you will have no reward from your Father who is in heaven.... When you give alms, do not let your left hand know what your right hand is doing, so that your alms may be in secret; and your Father who sees in secret will reward you." *(Mt 6:1, 3-4)*

No temptation has overtaken you that is not common to man. God is faithful, and he will not let you be tempted beyond your strength, but with the temptation will also provide the way of escape, that you may be able to endure it. *(1 Cor 10:13)*

Keep Me Young, Lord!

*What was wonderful
about childhood
is that anything in it
was a wonder.
It was not merely
a world of miracles;
it was a miraculous world.*

G. K. Chesterton

Keep Me Young, Lord!

Dear Lord,
I'm not exactly over the hill,
but I'm starting to think
that perhaps my "warranty" is expiring.
Muscles I was never aware of
are beginning to make their presence felt,
and attitudes I was determined never to assume
I am discovering to be the root
of some of my reactions.

Keep me young, Lord!
Young not because I'm offended
at the possibility of a wrinkle or two,
not because I mind a gray hair here and there,
but because I want to retain
a fresh outlook on life and love.
Grant me the wisdom that should come with age,
but also let me keep the wonder of youth, Lord!
Take away what makes me sometimes resent
the exuberance and energy
of my youngsters.
Let me remember my own youthful demands
and never let me squelch
the bubbling vibrancy of a new idea
or the excitement surrounding a new adventure.
Let me never grow stale, Lord.
Life is too short to waste it
on stubbornness or selfishness or fears.

In Your eternal youth,
You are the model for us all.
The members of Your kingdom are only those
who despite years have kept or reacquired
the simplicity, sincerity and freedom
of the children of God.

Bless the Lord, O my soul;
    and all that is within me, bless his holy name!
Bless the Lord, O my soul,
    and forget not all his benefits,
who forgives all your iniquity,
    who heals all your diseases,
who redeems your life from the Pit,
    who crowns you with steadfast love and mercy,
who satisfies you with good as long as you live
    so that your youth is renewed like the eagle's.

(Ps 103:1-5)

Thank You, Lord!

*The world is charged
with the grandeur of God.*
Gerard M. Hopkins

Thank You, Lord!

O God,
You never cease to amaze me.
How good You are to me
and how generous with Your gifts!
Thank You, Lord, for being You.
Your gifts are wonderful,
but You Yourself are the greatest Good.

Accept the thanksgiving I offer, Lord,
accompanied by a pledge to use Your gifts
to praise You and bless You.

With the joy that comes
from knowing I am loved by You,
I thank You for the great things
and the small,
Your works both mighty and hidden,
the things You've given
and those You've withheld for my good.
Thank You for the circumstances that shape me,
the sufferings that ennoble me,
the knowledge that draws me to You,
and especially the persons who are near and dear
to both of us, Lord.

O give thanks to the Lord, for he is good;
    his steadfast love endures for ever! *(Ps 118:1)*

It is good to give thanks to the Lord,
    to sing praises to your name, O Most High;
to declare your steadfast love in the morning,
    and your faithfulness by night,
to the music of the lute and the harp,
    to the melody of the lyre.
For you, O Lord, have made me glad by your work;
    at the works of your hands I sing for joy. *(Ps 92:1-4)*

Dieting

*In comparison
with the stars,
what is more trifling
a matter
than my dinner?*
St. Augustine

*He who has not
one master,
has many.*
St. Ambrose

Dieting

Dear Lord,
I'm beginning diet number 999 today.
If I'm lucky, I'll set a record
and keep it for at least a week.
But if past statistics indicate anything
it's this: I could certainly use some more will power.

The body and soul connection
is a genuine tug-of-war situation.
Even when I know that health and spirituality
counsel me to cut down on the extras,
I have a hard time staying convinced
when confronted with my favorites....
Isn't it a shame that someone You've "freed"
from slavery to sin and self
is still so blessedly bound
to pleasure and satisfaction?

I know that You have given us good things
as signs of Your love and care.
But I am aware too that self-discipline
is part of Your Gospel demand.
I turn to You, Lord, because I see so clearly
how weak I am without Your grace.
Dieting is not exactly pleasurable entertainment,
but it is a lot like athletics.
Saying "no" to some demands of the body
takes will power, stamina and determination.
Let me learn how to listen more to reason
than to appetite,
to be better fit physically
but even more importantly, spiritually.

Then Jesus told his disciples, "If any man would
come after me, let him deny himself and take up
his cross and follow me." *(Mt 16:24)*

Do you not know that in a race all the runners
compete, but only one receives the prize? So run
that you may obtain it. Every athlete exercises self-
control in all things. They do it to receive a
perishable wreath, but we an imperishable.

(1 Cor 9:24-25)

Let us run with perseverance the race that is set
before us, looking to Jesus the pioneer and perfecter
of our faith, who for the joy that was set before
him endured the cross, despising the shame, and is
seated at the right hand of the throne of God.

(Heb 12:1-2)

To Become Patient

May was never
the month of love
For May
is full of flowers;
But rather April,
wet by kind,
For love
is full of showers.

St. Robert Southwell

To Become Patient

Lord,
it's when things pile up
that I sometimes feel like I'm going
to either break up or blow up.
Why is it, Jesus, that when things go wrong
they seem to do so simultaneously?
Does Bobby have to come home
with a note about a smashed window
on the same day the stove has broken down
and I've gotten a flat tire and a parking ticket?

Yet deep down, Lord, I know my troubles
are far from being "earth shattering."
I guess that's the humiliating part of it all.
Things could be a lot worse.
There would be no broken-window note
if there weren't a Bobby,
no broken stove
if we weren't able to own one in the first place,
and no flat tire or ticket if we lacked a car.
All the alternatives are a lot worse
than the realities.

Patience is an expensive commodity, Lord.
I ask You to make me ready to pay the price.
I suppose it all boils down to either wanting
to do Your will or not wanting to do it.
Either I admit that You're in charge

and permit things for my own good
or I live a pretense
and become frustrated.

Take my hand, Lord.
You were willing to suffer and die
for love of me.
And You never complained about it.
Let me now at least accept these daily thorns
to make up for all the times I've offended You
and to show that the love I pray about
is a love that is real.

They who wait for the Lord shall renew their
    strength,
    they shall mount up with wings like eagles,
they shall run and not be weary,
    they shall walk and not faint. *(Is 40:31)*

Accept whatever is brought upon you,
    and in changes that humble you be patient.
For gold is tested in the fire,
    and acceptable men in the furnace of
    humiliation.
Trust in him, and he will help you;
    make your ways straight, and hope in him.

(Sir 2:4-6)

We know that in everything God works for good
with those who love him, who are called according
to his purpose. *(Rom 8:28)*

The Simple Things

We are all very simple;
it is when
we forget that,
that we go wrong.
R. H. Benson

Love but few
and simple things;
Simple life
much comfort brings.
Thomas à Kempis

The Simple Things

Lord,
the roller coaster of life
sometimes whisks me past
the most beautiful aspects of existence.
Slow me down, Lord, so that I may appreciate
the simple things that are tokens
of Your infinite love for Your children.

The delicate flowers, the burning sunsets,
the cool breezes,
the soft moonlight, the majestic mountains,
the childish giggle, the gentle embrace,
the morning kiss, the friendly conversation,
the sharing of memories, the pooling of dreams,
the smell of homecooking,
the glowing warmth of a family night—
the simple things that make life what it is.

I don't want to overlook Your gifts, Lord—
not even the smallest or most commonplace.
Give me the sensitivity and faith
to recognize Your creative, Fatherly hand
in every good thing around me.
And when I get wrapped up
in complicated concerns
and lose appreciation for the simple,
remind me, Lord, that it's You who are in charge
and that You care for all—
the great and the very, very small.

O Lord, our Lord,
    how majestic is your name in all the earth!
You whose glory above the heavens is chanted
    by the mouth of babes and infants. *(Ps 8:1-2)*

"Consider the lilies of the field, how they grow;
they neither toil nor spin; yet I tell you, even
Solomon in all his glory was not arrayed like one of
these. But if God so clothes the grass of the field,
which today is alive and tomorrow is thrown into
the oven, will he not much more clothe you, O men
of little faith?" *(Mt 6:28-30)*

The Three "P's" (Pets, Phones and Pots)

*And why, it is asked,
are there so many snares?
That we may not fly low,
but seek the things
that are above.*

St. John Chrysostom

The Three "P's"
(Pets, Phones and Pots)

Dear Lord,
granted You must have had a reason,
but could You please fill me in
on why there are so many species
of animals attractive to little boys?
Sometimes I wonder
if I'm raising future zoologists...
or if I should have bars installed
on all my windows
and save the expense of so many cages.
One more lizard in my bed and I'll....

Actually, while I'm complaining, Lord,
there are two other things
I could use Your help with
in trying to cope and keep my sanity.
The first of these major difficulties
was invented by Alexander Bell.
If only he'd known what he was beginning...
a life filled with bells, interruptions
and conversations you really never wanted to begin
and thought you'd never end.

The next area of difficulty is that of pots.
I've become sceptical
of cookingware "no-stick" signs:

they are symptomatic of modern "wishful thinking."
Who needs to be in the West to see the Rockies?
My kitchen has mountains right near the sink.

Well, Lord, I feel better already.
Sorry I held You up with my gripes.
But I do want You to know
that though I'm no heroine of patience,
telling You of my effort (or lack of it)
always helps me look at life in a better perspective.
With Your grace, I promise to try harder
to face slimy wildlife,
ringing gadgets and dirty cookingware
with poise and peace.

Maybe my three "P's" would be easier to live with
if I added a few more:
perspective, patience, promise, poise and peace.

For each of these, I need Your help
and I count on it with all my heart.

Learn where there is wisdom,
    where there is strength,
    where there is understanding,
That you may at the same time discern...
    where there is light for the eyes, and peace.

(Bar 3:14)

Betrayed

*Every sin
is more injury
to him who does it
than to him
who suffers it.*
St. Augustine

Betrayed

Dear Lord,
You have permitted that I come to taste
the gall of betrayal.
I never thought that such a thing
would scar the love of my marriage.
Nothing I can imagine
would inflict more suffering on me.

Yet I have come to realize
that You are my model in this trial.
You too were betrayed by one You loved.
You saw Your gifts accepted, then rejected.
Worse than the lash
was the scourge of Your apostles' infidelity.
You felt the stab of ingratitude
more keenly than the piercing of the nails.

O Lord, must it be this way?
Must we humans be so blind
to where true love is to be found?

From the cross You prayed
for Your crucifiers.
Each man and woman
has had a part in pounding those nails.
We are Your executioners.

Help me to see this time of intense pain
as an opportunity for suffering without bitterness,
for atoning in part for my own sins
and those of others.

I forgive my husband, Lord,
and I pray that Your grace will touch him.
He knows not what he is doing.

No matter what happens to my children or myself,
we are never really alone.
We have You as head of our house.
Be a Father to them, dear God,
and be a support to me
for I feel keenly the weight of this cross
and the weakness of my nature.
Help me to show
with a truly Christian attitude
that I consider my marriage
to be founded in You,
that I will never forsake
the sacred promises made
nor seek revenge in any manner,
nor look for healing and comfort
in any love other than Yours
or that which is rooted in Yours.
Let me and my children learn from this betrayal
the evil that is in sin,
so that we will never turn from You,
who are always faithful.

I waited patiently for the Lord;
    he inclined to me and heard my cry.

He drew me up from the desolate pit,
  out of the miry bog,
and set my feet upon a rock,
  making my steps secure.
He put a new song in my mouth,
  a song of praise to our God.
Many will see and fear,
  and put their trust in the Lord.
Blessed is the man who makes
  the Lord his trust. *(Ps 40:1-4)*

[Jesus] withdrew from them about a stone's throw, and knelt down and prayed, "Father, if you are willing, remove this cup from me; nevertheless not my will, but yours, be done." *(Lk 22:41-42)*

As Christmas Approaches

The birthday of the Lord is the birthday of peace.

St. Leo the Great

As Christmas Approaches

Lord Jesus,
soon we will celebrate the wonder
of Your birth.
Every time I glance at the tree
and look at the nativity set,
I am filled with the desire to just stop
and ponder the meaning of Your coming.

Yet, Lord, I feel incapable
of inner peace and silence.
I run from store to store,
looking for bargains,
trying to stretch dollars—
which are becoming, by the way,
an extinct species here—
and neglecting all too often
the spirit of Advent.

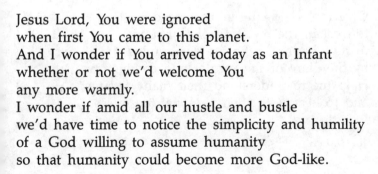

Jesus Lord, You were ignored
when first You came to this planet.
And I wonder if You arrived today as an Infant
whether or not we'd welcome You
any more warmly.
I wonder if amid all our hustle and bustle
we'd have time to notice the simplicity and humility
of a God willing to assume humanity
so that humanity could become more God-like.

During a still night, You came—
heralded by the angels
and noticed only by the lowly of this earth.

Help me, Jesus, to be like those shepherds.
I, too, have a "flock."
Let me look after them,
attend to their needs,
but never be so busy that I miss out
on Your coming into my life.

Give me the patience and fortitude I need
to shop without resenting people who are rude,
or who take the last of the item I wanted,
or who pull into the parking space I was eyeing.
Let me be inspired by Your example:
there was no room for You in the inn,
yet You did not complain;
You were ignored by most people,
yet You did not resent this,
but considered humility and lowliness
the most regal of honors.

Give me, Lord, the grace I need
to explain the meaning of Christmas
to my children, who are surrounded
by the glare of the secular and commercial.
Help me to understand their many "wants,"
and to bear with their seasonal tenseness.

Most of all, Lord,
enable me to make Christmas a way of life,
a welcoming attitude that always has room
for the spiritual
and always has time to give of self
for the good of others.

Come, Lord, into the world.
Come to this family in a special way.
Make us eager for Your coming
and more worthy to receive You,
our Gift from the Father.

While gentle silence enveloped all things,
and night in its swift course was now half gone,
your all-powerful word leaped from heaven,
    from the royal throne,
into the midst of the land that was doomed....

(Wis 18:14-15)

The true light that enlightens every man was
coming into the world. He was in the world, and
the world was made through him, yet the world
knew him not. He came to his own home, and his
own people received him not. But to all who
received him, who believed in his name, he gave
power to become children of God....

And the Word became flesh and dwelt among
us, full of grace and truth; we have beheld his
glory, glory as of the only Son from the Father. And
from his fullness have we all received, grace upon
grace. *(Jn 1:9-12, 14, 16)*

To Live Easter

*The light of Christ
is an endless day
that knows no night.*

St. Maximus of Turin

To Live Easter

Lord,
the shadows of Your passion
have lengthened during Lent.
But today You fill us with joy
and delight us
with the brilliance of the Easter dawn.

My children have dutifully kept
(more or less)
their Lenten resolutions to give up
their favorite TV program
and some sweets or other dish.
I've often looked at inner battles
reflected on youthful faces
and marvelled at the power of Your grace.
I know that they've not always won the battles,
but the fact that they even tried to fight them
in this modern day and age
makes me grateful for the youngsters
You've entrusted to my husband and me.

There have been some battles for us adults, too.
Chocolate and TV have not been
the greatest "pulls,"
I must admit.
The satisfaction of winning a discussion
or retaliating for an unkind word
or answering curtly to an ill-timed request
or passing up the opportunity

to go out of my way for others
can be much more appealing,
but so inappropriate for such a holy season as Lent.

I am sorry, Lord, for the times
I have failed to live
in a spirit of charity and self-sacrifice.
When I look upon Your cross,
I am filled with sorrow
but also with hope
and the realization that Your love
is far greater than my weakness.

Let me, Lord, grow in the desire
to die to self,
so that I can truly live in You.
Cast out the shadows of my sins
and fill me with the radiance of Your life and light.
Turn me away from the "thirty pieces of silver"
by which I can sell out on You
for the sake of my comfort,
or selfishness
or pride.

Easter—an empty tomb and a plentiful life,
an end of suffering
and a beginning of profound joy.
Let me live the Easter spirit, Lord,
by setting my heart on the things above
and facing the Calvary of life
confident that resurrection will follow.

In the beginning was the Word, and the Word was
with God, and the Word was God. In him was life,

and the life was the light of men. The light shines in the darkness, and the darkness has not overcome it. *(Jn 1:1, 4-5)*

We were buried with [Christ] by baptism into death, so that as Christ was raised from the dead by the glory of the Father, we too might walk in newness of life.

For if we have been united with him in a death like his, we shall certainly be united with him in a resurrection like his. We know that our old self was crucified with him so that the sinful body might be destroyed, and we might no longer be enslaved to sin. If we have died with Christ, we believe that we shall also live with him. *(Rom 6:4-6, 8)*

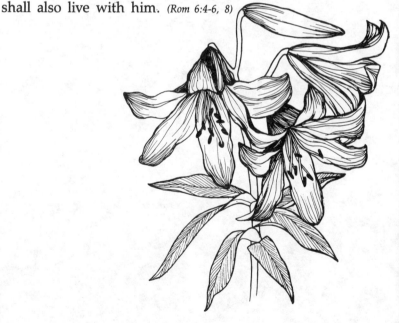

When the Children Grow Up

*The beloved may be absent
or present,
but love stays on.*
St. Thomas Aquinas

When the Children Grow Up

Father,
I feel so alone today.
For so many years now
I have heard pattering feet,
then childish giggles,
then teenage music,
then wedding plans,
and now...
now there is only silence.
The children are all gone;
even the cat has strayed.
I feel so alone.

Yet I know that this, too, is part of Your plan.
You help us in times like this
to grow closer to You,
to appreciate more the unchangeableness
of Your presence and of Your love.
You NEVER go away.

My role in the lives of my children
is a different one now.
Help me never to forget that, Father.
In permitting me to give them life
You did not intend that I should pretend
to dominate the direction of their lives.
Lead me to trust their decisions,
to counsel when love and prudence require it,
and to confide them daily to Your care.

After all, You love them more than I ever could.
You watch over them more closely still
than I ever did even when they were in the cradle.

And speaking of cradles, Lord,
the sooner grandchildren come
the happier I'll be.
Perhaps the second round of pattering feet
will bring as much or even more joy
than did the first.

Lord, you have been our dwelling place
    in all generations.
Before the mountains were brought forth,
    or ever you had formed the earth and the
        world,
    from everlasting to everlasting you are God.

You turn men back to the dust,
    and say, "Turn back, O children of men!"
For a thousand years in your sight
    are but as yesterday when it is past,
    or as a watch in the night. (Ps 90:1-4)

They will perish, but you endure;
    they will all wear out like a garment.
You change them like raiment, and they pass away;
    but you are the same, and your years have no
        end. (Ps 102:26-27)

ST. PAUL BOOK & MEDIA CENTERS
OPERATED BY THE DAUGHTERS OF ST. PAUL

ALASKA
750 West 5th Ave., Anchorage, AK 99501 **907-272-8183.**
CALIFORNIA
3908 Sepulveda Blvd., Culver City, CA 90230 **213-202-8144.**
1570 Fifth Ave. (at Cedar Street), San Diego, CA 92101 **619-232-1442.**
46 Geary Street, San Francisco, CA 94108 **415-781-5180.**
FLORIDA
Coral Park Shopping Center, 9808 S.W. 8 St., Miami, FL 33174
305-559-6715; 305-559-6716.
HAWAII
1143 Bishop Street, Honolulu, HI 96813 **808-521-2731.**
ILLINOIS
172 North Michigan Ave., Chicago, IL 60601 **312-346-4228; 312-346-3240.**
LOUISIANA
423 Main Street, Baton Rouge, LA 70802 **504-343-4057; 504-336-1504.**
4403 Veterans Memorial Blvd., Metairie, LA 70006 **504-887-7631;**
504-887-0113.
MASSACHUSETTS
50 St. Paul's Ave., Jamaica Plain, Boston, MA 02130 **617-522-8911.**
Rte. 1, 450 Providence Hwy., Dedham, MA 02026 **617-326-5385.**
MISSOURI
1001 Pine Street (at North 10th), St. Louis, MO 63101 **314-621-0346.**
NEW JERSEY
Hudson Mall, Route 440 and Communipaw Ave.,
Jersey City, NJ 07304 **201-433-7740.**
NEW YORK
625 East 187th Street, Bronx, NY 10458 **212-584-0440.**
59 East 43rd Street, New York, NY 10017 **212-986-7580.**
78 Fort Place, Staten Island, NY 10301 **718-447-5071; 718-447-5086.**
OHIO
616 Walnut Street, Cincinnati, OH 45202 **513-421-5733.**
2105 Ontario Street (at Prospect Ave.), Cleveland, OH 44115
216-621-9427.
PENNSYLVANIA
1719 Chestnut Street, Philadelphia, PA 19103 **215-568-2638;**
215-864-0991.
SOUTH CAROLINA
243 King Street, Charleston, SC 29401 **803-577-0175.**
TEXAS
114 Main Plaza, San Antonio, TX 78205 **512-224-8101.**
VIRGINIA
1025 King Street, Alexandria, VA 22314 **703-549-3806.**
WASHINGTON
2301 Second Ave. (at Bell), Seattle, WA 98121 **206-441-4100.**
CANADA
3022 Dufferin Street, Toronto 395, Ontario, Canada.